Houghton Mifflin
English

Shirley Haley-James   John Warren Stewig

Marcus T. Ballenger   Jacqueline L. Chaparro   Nancy C. Millett
June Grant Shane   C. Ann Terry

HOUGHTON   MIFFLIN   COMPANY   BOSTON

Atlanta   Dallas   Geneva, Illinois   Palo Alto   Princeton   Toronto

Acknowledgments

Jamaica's Find by Juanita Havill, illustrations by Anne Sibley O'Brien. Text copyright © 1986 by Juanita Havill. Illustrations copyright © 1986 by Anne Sibley O'Brien. Reprinted with permission of Houghton Mifflin Company.

Mr. Benn-Red Knight by David McKee. Copyright © 1968 by David McKee. Reprinted with permission of McGraw-Hill Book Company, and Dobson Books Limited.

The publisher has made every effort to locate each owner of the copyrighted material reprinted here. Any information enabling the publisher to rectify or credit any reference is welcome.

Credits

Illustrations

Anthony Accardo: 66, 67, 68
Mary Jane Begin: 54-55
Lorinda Cauley: 93, 94, 95
Maxie Chambliss: 7, 9, 11, 17, 19, 21, 25, 29, 31, 33, 35, 37, 44, 47, 56, 57, 58, 59, 63, 69, 86, 89, 91, 101, 113, 114, 120, 126, *Classifying Game*
Doug Cushman: 115
Judy Filippo: 76, 90, 104, 118, 119, 121, 122, 123, 124, 125
Judith Griffith: 78, 79, 80, 81
Marilyn Janovitz: 60, 61, 65
Carol Leeson: 83, 84, 99, 100, 109, 116, 117
David McKee: 107
Anne Sibley O'Brien: 41, 42
Jan Palmer: 43, 48, 49, 50, 51, 52, 74, 75, 96, 97
Paul Sances: 40-41 (borders), 106-107 (borders)
Susan Spellman: 13, 15, 17, 23, 27, 45, 46, 53, 62, 64, 70, 71, 72, 73, 85, 87, 88, 102, 103, 105, 108, 111, *Same-Different Puzzles, Left-Right Game, First-Next-Last Game*

Photographs

6 Nancy Sheehan.   39 Bonnie Unsworth.   40 Michal Heron.   44 (left) Olmsted Studios.   44 (right) John Lei/Stock Boston   53 (top) Gus Schonefeld/Berg & Assoc.   53 (top center) Russ Lappa.   53 (bottom, bottom center) Victoria Beller-Smith.   54 David and Linda Phillips.   66 Richard Hutchings.   77 (left) Victoria Beller-Smith.   77 (right) Michal Heron.   78 Charles Gupton/The Stock Market.   82 Tom Stack/Tom Stack & Assoc.   82 Don & Pat Valenti/Tom Stack & Assoc.   92 R. Solomon/Leo deWys Inc.   98 Nancy Sheehan.   106 Marjorie Pickens.   110, 112 Nancy Sheehan.

Cover Photographs

Cover and title page photograph: Ron Kimball

The photograph shows tigers from the Los Angeles Zoo in Los Angeles, California.

Back cover: Jon Chomitz

1998 Impression
Copyright © 1990 by Houghton Mifflin Company. All rights reserved.

Printed in U.S.A.

ISBN: 0-395-48089-2

KLMN-WC-998

Table of Contents

Part One: Readiness

Activity Worksheets for Posters 1–16   **6**

• Activity Worksheet for Poster 1	Theme: Birthdays	**7**
• Activity Worksheet for Poster 2	Theme: Stories and Rhymes	**9**
• Activity Worksheet for Poster 3	Theme: Safety	**11**
• Activity Worksheet for Poster 4	Theme: Community Helpers	**13**
• Activity Worksheet for Poster 5	Theme: Weather	**15**
• Activity Worksheet for Poster 6	Theme: Shapes	**17**
• Activity Worksheet for Poster 7	Theme: Things That Grow	**19**
• Activity Worksheet for Poster 8	Theme: Puppets	**21**
• Activity Worksheet for Poster 9	Theme: The Supermarket	**23**
• Activity Worksheet for Poster 10	Theme: Camouflage	**25**
• Activity Worksheet for Poster 11	Theme: Country and City	**27**
• Activity Worksheet for Poster 12	Theme: Music in Art	**29**
• Activity Worksheet for Poster 13	Theme: Under the Sea	**31**
• Activity Worksheet for Poster 14	Theme: The Circus	**33**
• Activity Worksheet for Poster 15	Theme: The Art Museum	**35**
• Activity Worksheet for Poster 16	Theme: Butterflies	**37**

Part Two: Skill Lessons

Units 1–6 and Student's Resource Book   **39**

Unit 1   **40**

Our Families and Ourselves

1 Literature: Characters from a Story	**42**
2 Listening: Following One-Step Directions	**43**
3 Speaking: Using the Telephone	**44**
4 Thinking: Same and Different	**45**
5 Writing Process Readiness: Adding Details	**47**
6 Grammar: Listening to Telling Sentences	**48**
7 Grammar: Using Telling Sentences	**49**
8 Grammar: Listening to Asking Sentences	**50**
9 Grammar: Using Asking Sentences	**51**
10 Vocabulary: in, on, under, over	**52**
11 Study Skills: Signs	**53**

Unit 2   54

Animal Friends

1 **Literature:** Listening for Rhyme   56
2 **Listening:** Following Two-Step Directions   57
3 **Listening:** Listening for Information   58
4 **Speaking:** Completing Sentences   59
5 **Thinking:** Classifying by Color or Shape   60
6 **Writing Process Readiness:** Drawing and Describing   61
7 **Grammar:** Naming Words for People   62
8 **Grammar:** Naming Words for Animals   63
9 **Vocabulary:** happy, sad, angry   64
10 **Study Skills:** Left and Right   65

Unit 3   66

At School and at Play

1 **Literature:** Recalling Story Sequence   68
2 **Listening:** Following Three-Step Directions   69
3 **Speaking:** Telling a Story   70
4 **Thinking:** first, next, last   71
5 **Writing Process Readiness:** Completing a Story   72
6 **Grammar:** Naming Words: Places, Things   73
7 **Grammar:** One and More Than One   74
8 **Vocabulary:** beside, between, behind, in front of   75
9 **Study Skills:** Learning My Letters   76
10 **Study Skills:** Following Picture Directions   77

Unit 4   78

Places Near and Far

1 **Literature:** Recalling Story Setting   80
2 **Listening:** Predicting an Outcome   81
3 **Speaking:** Discussing Places   82
4 **Thinking:** Classifying   83
5 **Writing Process Readiness:** A Story About Me   84
6 **Grammar:** Action Words   85
7 **Grammar:** More Action Words   86
8 **Grammar:** Matching Action Words   87
9 **Grammar:** Action Words in Sentences   88
10 **Vocabulary:** yesterday, today, tomorrow   89
11 **Study Skills:** Learning My Letters   90
12 **Study Skills:** Practicing for a Test   91

Unit 5 — 92

The World Around Us

1 **Literature:** Sound Words — 94
2 **Listening:** Listening for Specific Details — 95
3 **Speaking:** Choral Speaking — 96
4 **Thinking:** Cause and Effect — 97
5 **Writing Process Readiness:** Making a Book — 98
6 **Grammar:** Describing Color, Shape, Size — 101
7 **Grammar:** Comparing and Describing — 102
8 **Vocabulary:** Opposites — 103
9 **Study Skills:** Learning My Letters — 104
10 **Study Skills:** The Seasons of the Year — 105

Unit 6 — 106

Real and Make-Believe

1 **Literature:** Real and Make-Believe — 108
2 **Listening:** Drawing Conclusions — 109
3 **Speaking:** Making and Using Puppets — 110
4 **Thinking:** Solving Problems — 111
5 **Writing Process Readiness:** Making a Book — 112
6 **Grammar:** Describing Smells and Tastes — 115
7 **Grammar:** Describing How Things Sound and Feel — 116
8 **Vocabulary:** top, middle, bottom — 117
9 **Study Skills:** Learning My Letters — 118
10 **Study Skills:** ABC Order — 120

Student's Resource Book — 121

Picture Dictionary — 121

Colors — 126

■ **Index** — 127

Punchouts
  Games
    Same-Different Puzzles
    The Left-Right Game
    The First-Next-Last Game
    The Classifying Game
  Book Covers
    My Story About Me
    My Make-Believe Story

Part One: Readiness

Activity Worksheets for Posters 1–16

Name _____

Activity Worksheet for Poster 1

Name _Emily_____

Birthday _December 10th_____

Children color, cut out, and wear birthday badges.

Name _____

Activity Worksheet for Poster 2

Children color, cut out, and assemble a nursery rhyme book.

Activity Worksheet
Poster 2

9

Name _____

Activity Worksheet for Poster 3

Children color, cut out, and use simple signs to give
nonverbal directions.

Name

Activity Worksheet for Poster 4

Children color, paste, and cut out cards for use in a matching game.

Activity Worksheet for Poster 5

Children color, cut, and paste pictures in place.

Activity Worksheet for Poster 6

Children cut, paste, and color shapes to create a house or
other object of their choice.

Activity Worksheet
Poster 6

17

Name _____

Activity Worksheet for Poster 7

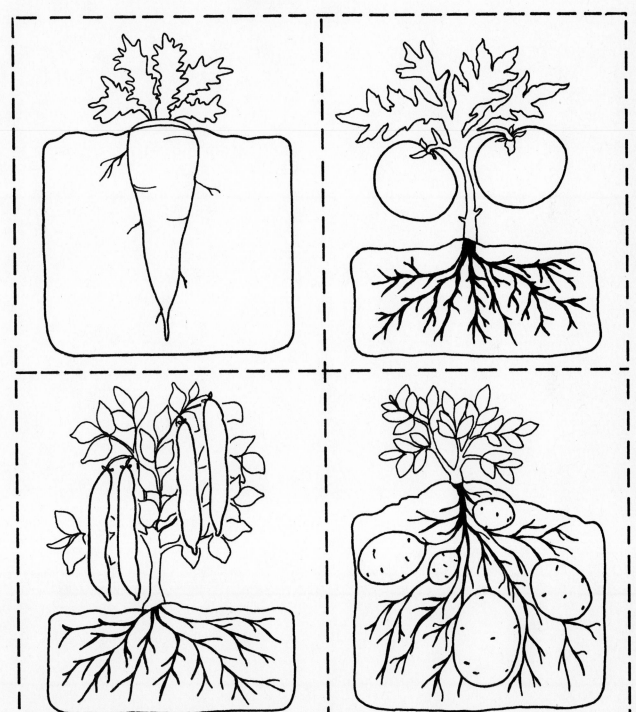

Children color and cut to make garden labels.

Activity Worksheet
Poster 7

19

Name

Activity Worksheet for Poster 8

Children color and cut to make simple puppets.

Activity Worksheet for Poster 9

1

2

3

4

5

6

Children color, cut out, and assemble a recipe booklet.

Activity Worksheet for Poster 10

Children find and color the hidden animals.

Name

Activity Worksheet for Poster 11

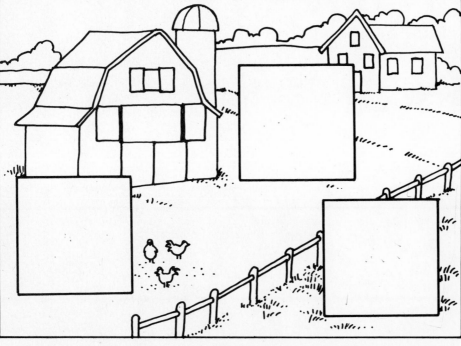

Children color, cut, and paste pictures in place.

Activity Worksheet
Poster 11

27

Name _____

Activity Worksheet for Poster 12

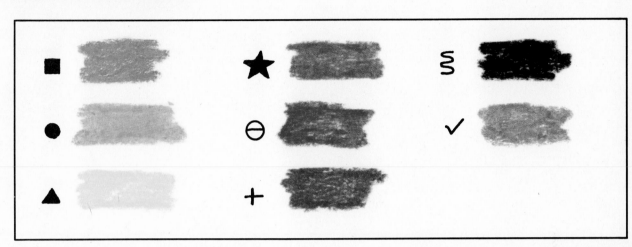

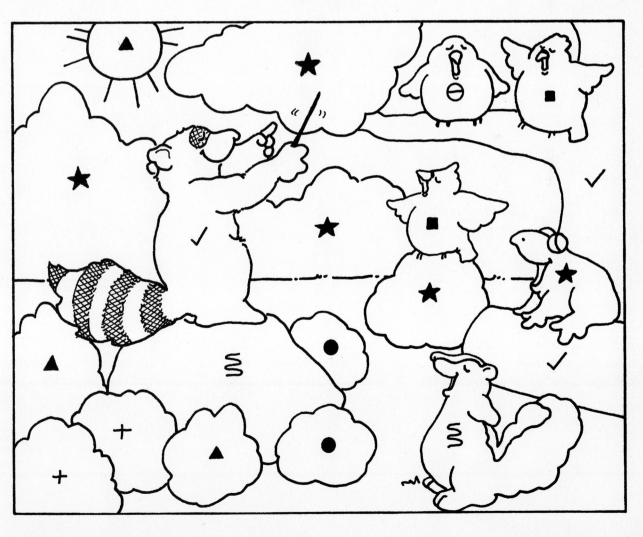

Children color sections of the picture according to the color key.

Activity Worksheet
Poster 12   **29**

Activity Worksheet for Poster 13

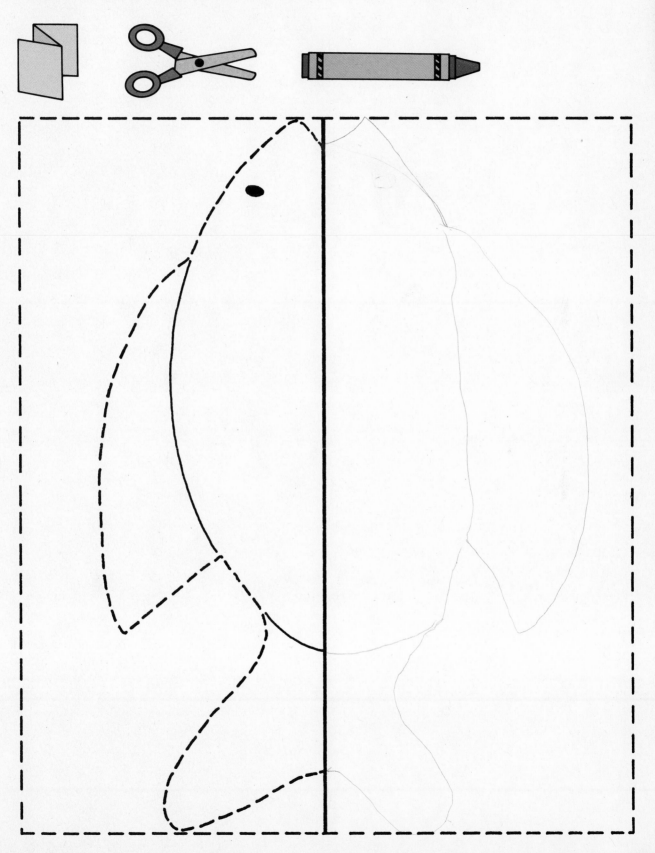

Children fold, cut, and color to create a paper fish.

Name _____

Activity Worksheet for Poster 14

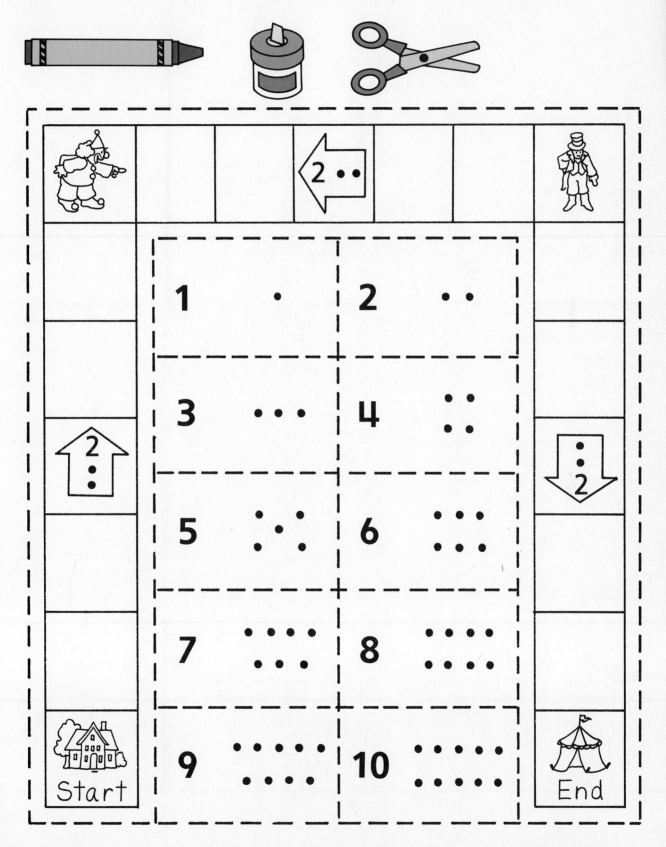

Children make and use a simple counting game.

Activity Worksheet for Poster 15

Children color, cut, and paste pictures in place.

Name _____

Activity Worksheet for Poster 16

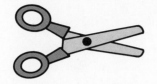

Children color, cut, and fold to make a butterfly.

Activity Worksheet
Poster 16 **37**

Part Two: Skill Lessons

Units 1–6 and Student's Resource Book

Jamaica's Find

by Juanita Havill

1 LITERATURE
Characters from a Story

Children circle pictures of characters from a story.

Name

2 LISTENING
Following One-Step Directions

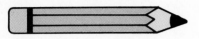

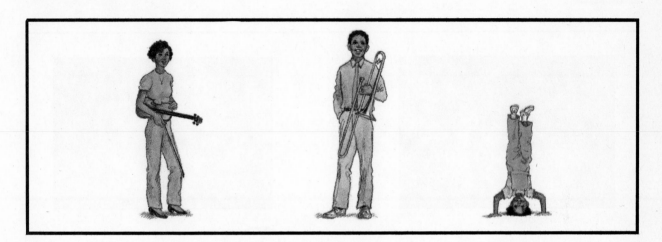

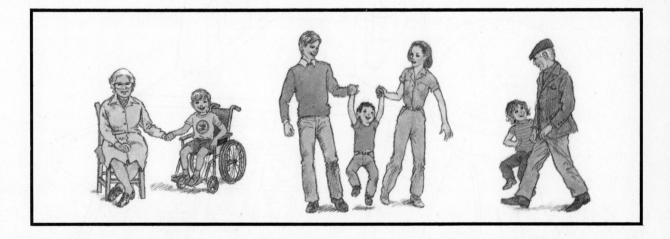

Children listen and mark named pictures according to
teacher's one-step oral directions.

Name

3 SPEAKING
Using the Telephone

Unit 1
Speaking

Children discuss how to use the telephone and color the
picture according to teacher's instructions.

Name

4 THINKING
Same and Different

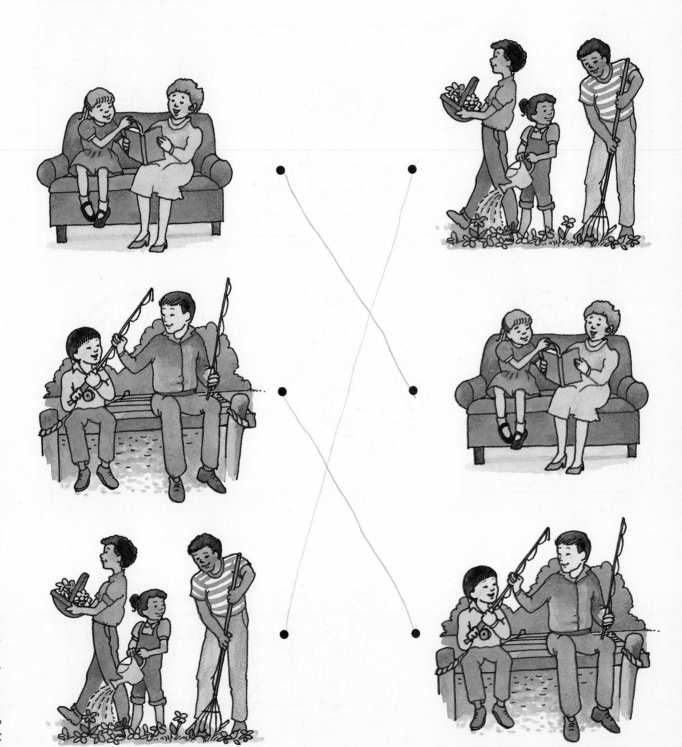

Children draw lines between pictures that are the same.

Name

Same and Different continued

Unit 1
Thinking

Children color the picture in each row that is different.

5 WRITING PROCESS READINESS
Adding Details

Children follow steps of the Writing Process to complete
a picture. They then dictate a description of the picture.

6 GRAMMAR
Listening to Telling Sentences

Children listen to telling sentences and color shapes beside corresponding pictures according to teacher's instructions.

7 GRAMMAR
Using Telling Sentences

Children discuss the picture and dictate telling sentences about it.

Name _____

8 GRAMMAR
Listening to Asking Sentences

Children answer questions by marking pictures with an **X**.

9 GRAMMAR
Using Asking Sentences

Children discuss the pictures and dictate questions that
the people might be asking.

Name

10 VOCABULARY
in, on, under, over

Unit 1
Vocabulary

Children circle objects in positions indicated by teacher.

11 STUDY SKILLS
Signs

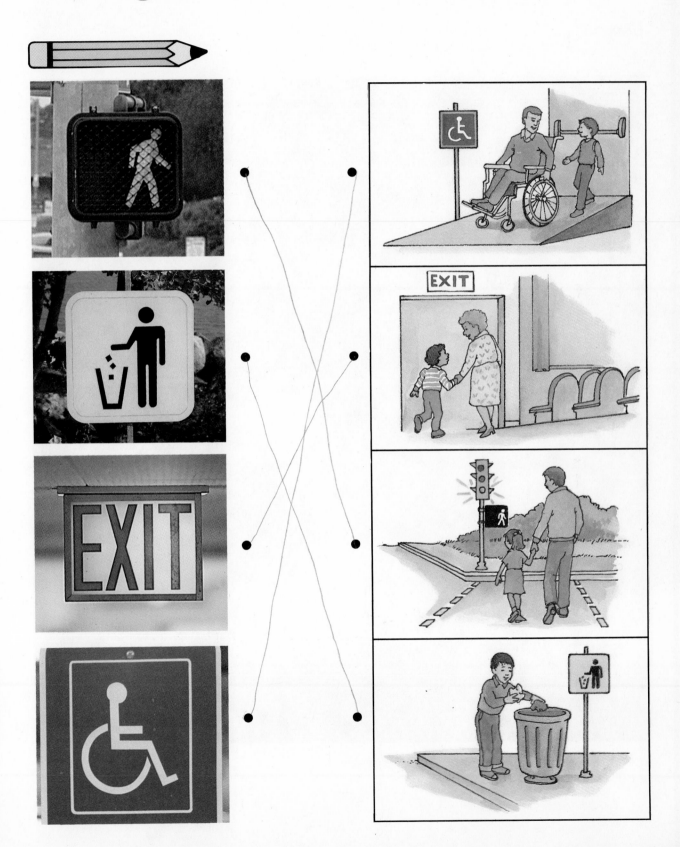

Children draw lines from signs to matching pictures.

Animal Friends

Over in the
Meadow

1 LITERATURE
Listening for Rhyme

Children color the two pictures in each row that illustrate rhyming words.

2 LISTENING
Following Two-Step Directions

Children listen and mark circles under pictures according to teacher's two-step oral directions.

3 LISTENING
Listening for Information

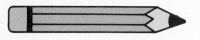

Children listen for details and circle illustrations
that accurately picture a hippopotamus.

4 SPEAKING
Completing Sentences

Children complete sentences read aloud by responding
orally and by circling the correct picture in each row.

Name _____

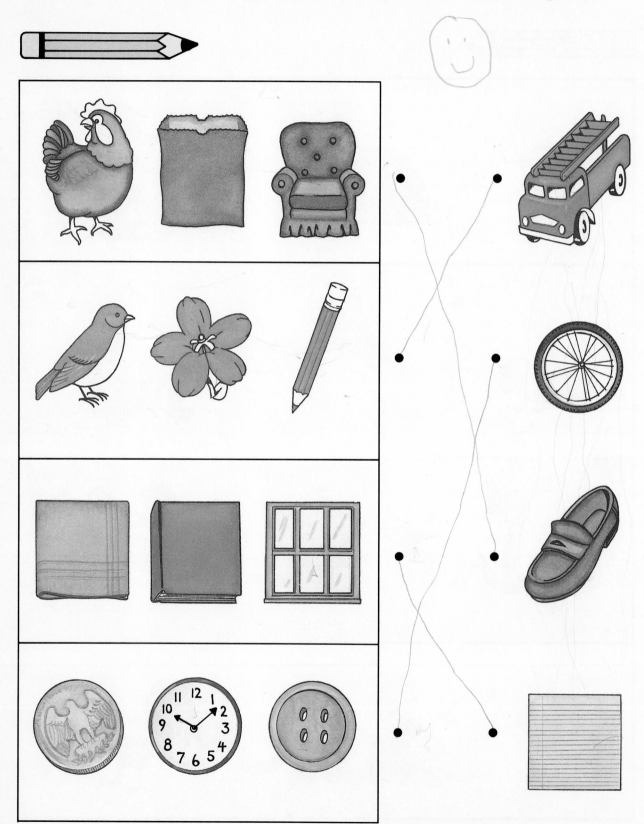

Children study groups of objects. They draw a line to another object that belongs in each group.

Name

6 WRITING PROCESS READINESS
Drawing and Describing

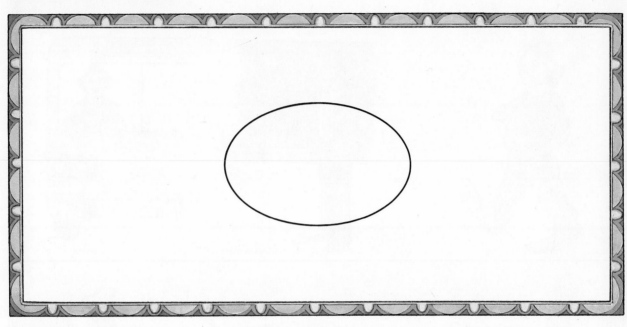

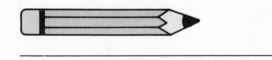

Children follow steps of the Writing Process to complete
a picture. They then dictate a description of the picture.

7 GRAMMAR
Naming Words for People

Children mark pictures of people according to teacher's instructions.

Name

8 GRAMMAR
Naming Words for Animals

Children color pictures of animals according to teacher's instructions.

Name _____

happy, sad, angry

Children draw lines from pictures to faces with correct expressions.

10 STUDY SKILLS
Left and Right

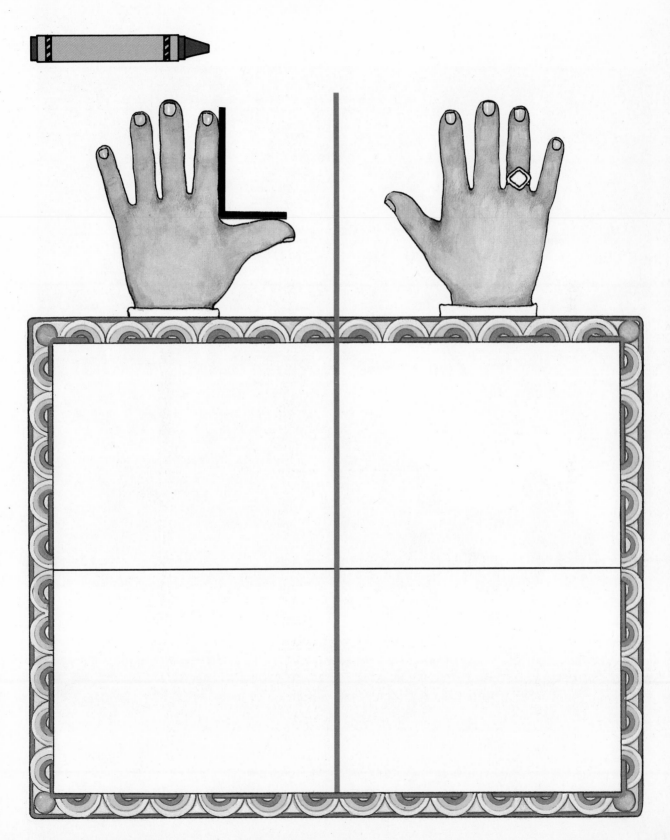

Children draw simple pictures on left or right according
to teacher's instructions.

At School and at Play

The Blanket That Had to Go

by Nancy Evans Cooney

1 LITERATURE
Recalling Story Sequence

Children color boxes according to teacher's instructions to show correct story sequence.

Name _____

2 LISTENING
Following Three-Step Directions

Children listen and follow teacher's three-step oral directions to complete the clown.

3 SPEAKING
Telling a Story

Children discuss pictures and create a class story to accompany them.

4 THINKING
first, next, last

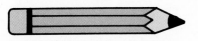

Children think about the pictures in each row and mark them to show what happened first, next, and last.

Name _____

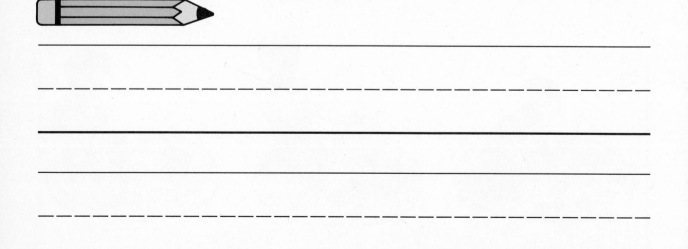

Children follow steps of the Writing Process to draw an
ending for a story. They then dictate the story ending.

Name _____

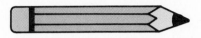

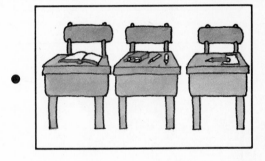

Children identify the pictures. They match places with pictures of things that would be found there.

7 GRAMMAR
One and More Than One

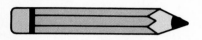

Children mark groups of one and more than one
according to teacher's instructions.

Name

beside, between, behind, in front of

Children color clothing of people in stated positions according to teacher's instructions.

9 STUDY SKILLS
Learning My Letters

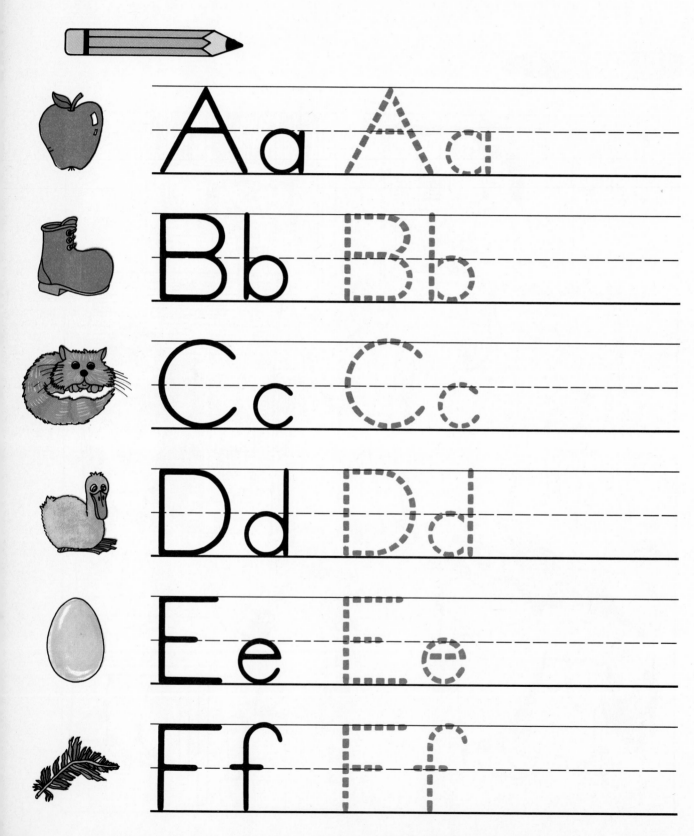

Children identify, trace, and copy upper- and lower-case letters.

Name _____

10 STUDY SKILLS
Following Picture Directions

Children discuss and follow illustrated directions to complete a simple project.

Places Near and Far

Tikki Tikki Tembo
retold by Arlene Mosel

Name _____

1 LITERATURE
Recalling Story Setting

Children color a picture in each row showing one of the settings from a story.

Name

**Children listen to an unfinished story and predict
outcome by coloring one of the pictures.**

Name

Children discuss photos and what appears in them. They draw pictures of other things that might be found in each place.

Name

4 THINKING Classifying

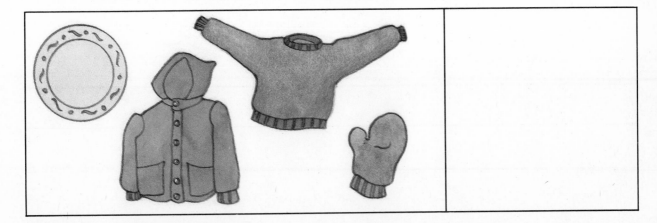

Children think about the objects in each row. They circle
those that belong together and draw an additional
object for each group.

Name _____

5 WRITING PROCESS READINESS
A Story About Me

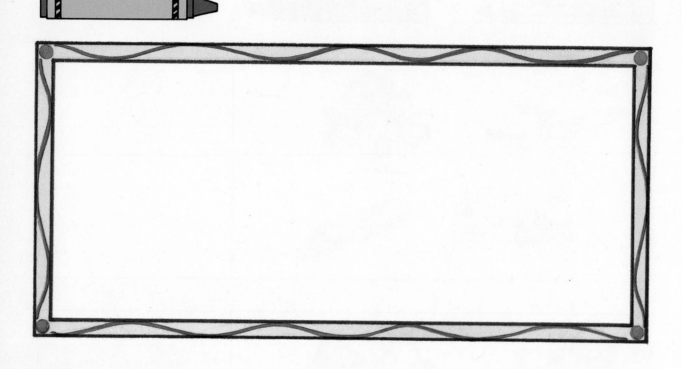

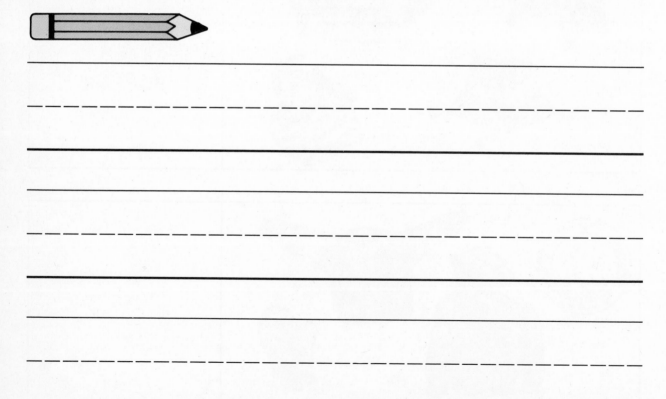

Children follow steps of the Writing Process to illustrate a story. They then dictate the story, or write it, using invented spelling.

6 GRAMMAR
Action Words

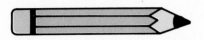

Children mark pictures illustrating action words
according to teacher's instructions.

Name

7 GRAMMAR
More Action Words

Children color pictures of animals performing actions named by teacher.

8 GRAMMAR
Matching Action Words

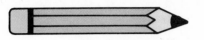

Children match pictures illustrating named actions
according to teacher's instructions.

9 GRAMMAR
Action Words in Sentences

Children complete sentences read aloud by circling the
correct picture in each row.

Name _____

10 VOCABULARY
yesterday, today, tomorrow

Children discuss pictures illustrating time order. They draw pictures to complete the sequences.

Name

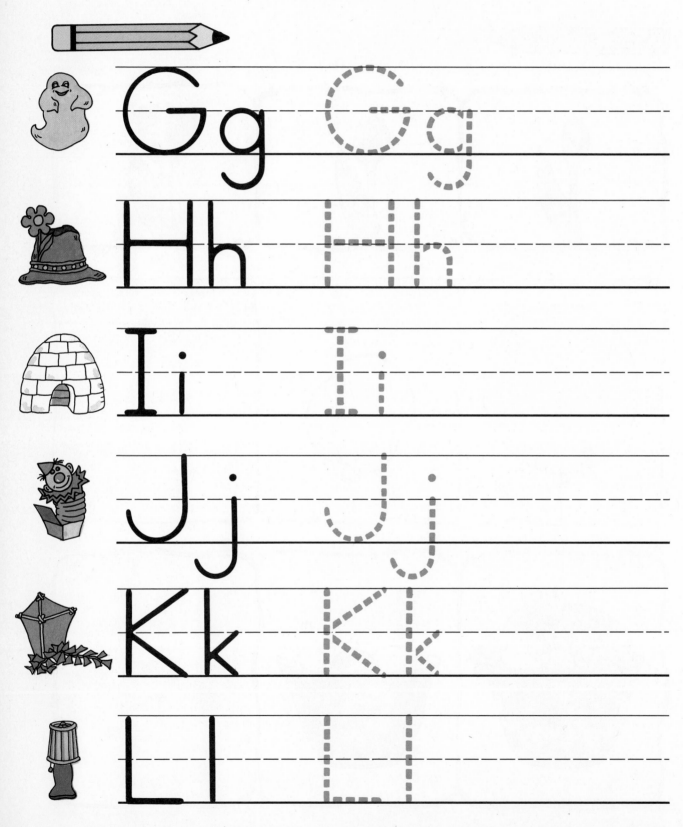

Children identify, trace, and copy upper- and lower-case letters.

Name _____

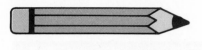

12 STUDY SKILLS
Practicing for a Test

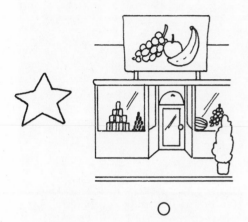  

○ ○ ○

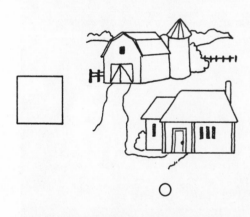 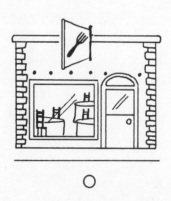 

○ ○ ○

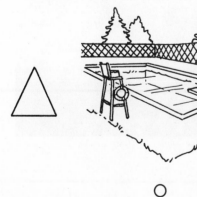  

○ ○ ○

Children practice for standardized tests by using a pencil
to fill in circles under named places.

The World Around Us

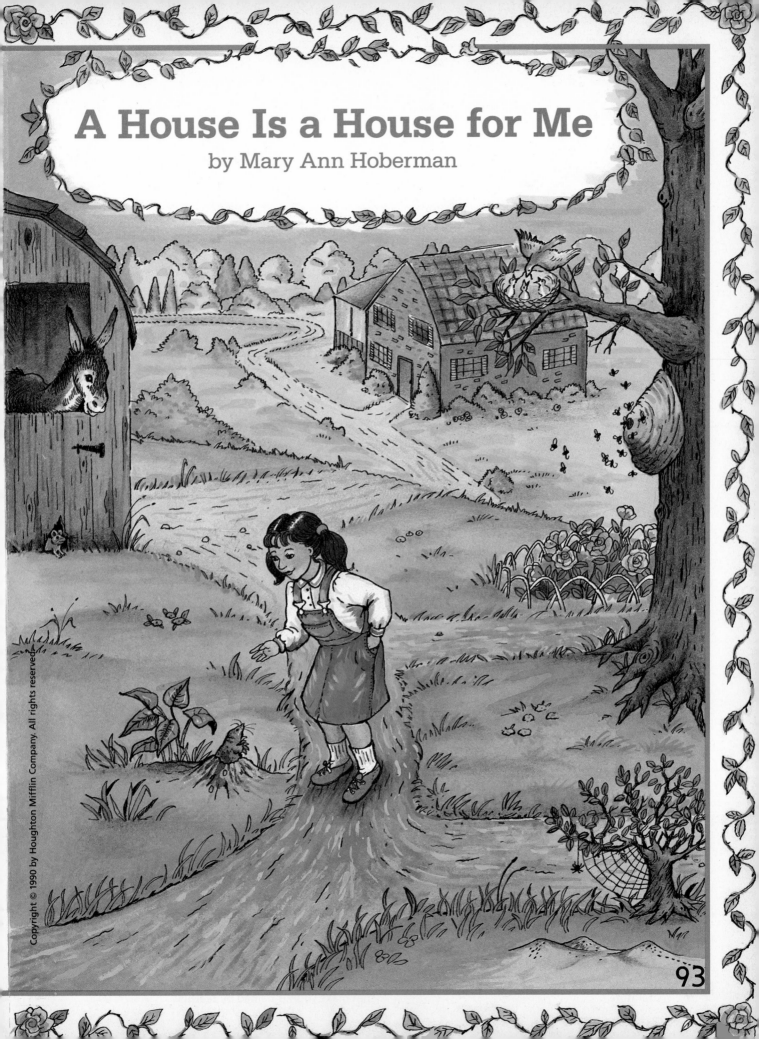

A House Is a House for Me
by Mary Ann Hoberman

1 LITERATURE
Sound Words

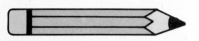

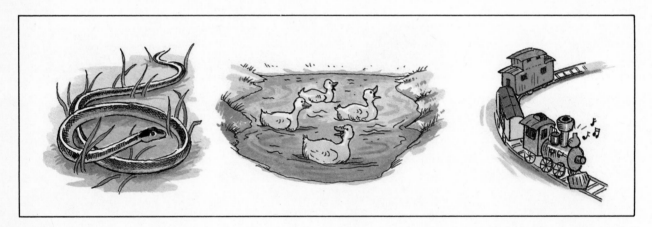

Children listen to a story and mark animals and objects that make sounds named by teacher.

2 LISTENING
Listening for Specific Details

Children listen to descriptive sentences and circle the correct pictures.

3 SPEAKING
Choral Speaking

Children participate in the choral reading of a poem.

4 THINKING
Cause and Effect

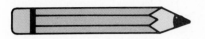

   •   •

   •   •

   •   •

   •   •

Children think about and match pictures of causes and effects.

Name

5 WRITING PROCESS READINESS
Making a Book

Children follow steps of the Writing Process to draw parts of a story. They then dictate the story, or write it, using invented spelling.

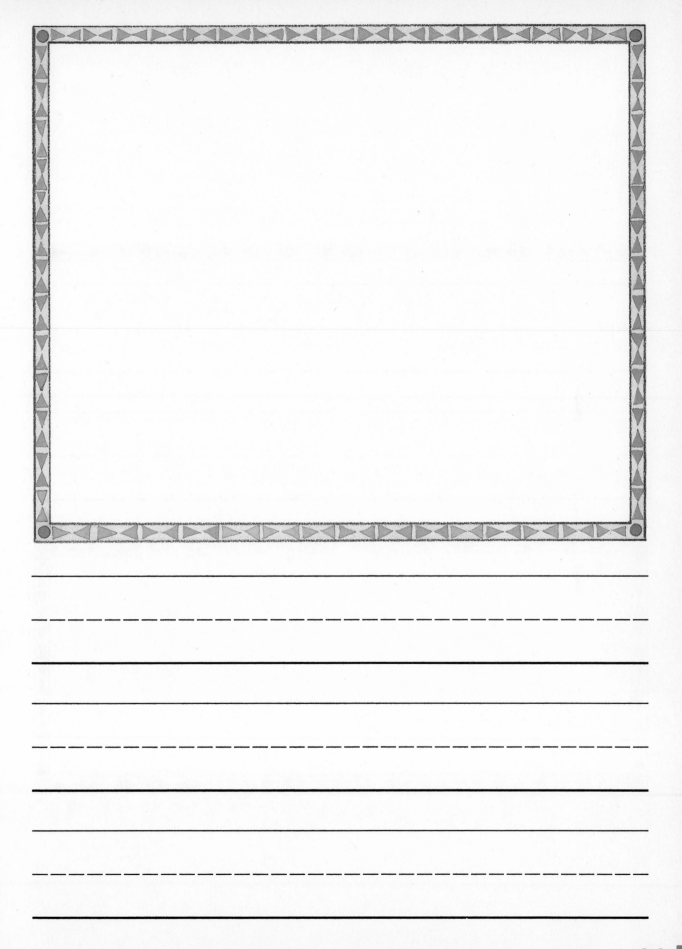

Name

6 GRAMMAR
Describing Color, Shape, Size

Children identify and color pictures described by their teacher.

Unit 5
Grammar **101**

7 GRAMMAR
Comparing and Describing

Children discuss and color pictures illustrating describing words named by teacher.

Name

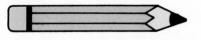

Children identify and match pictures illustrating opposites.

9 STUDY SKILLS
Learning My Letters

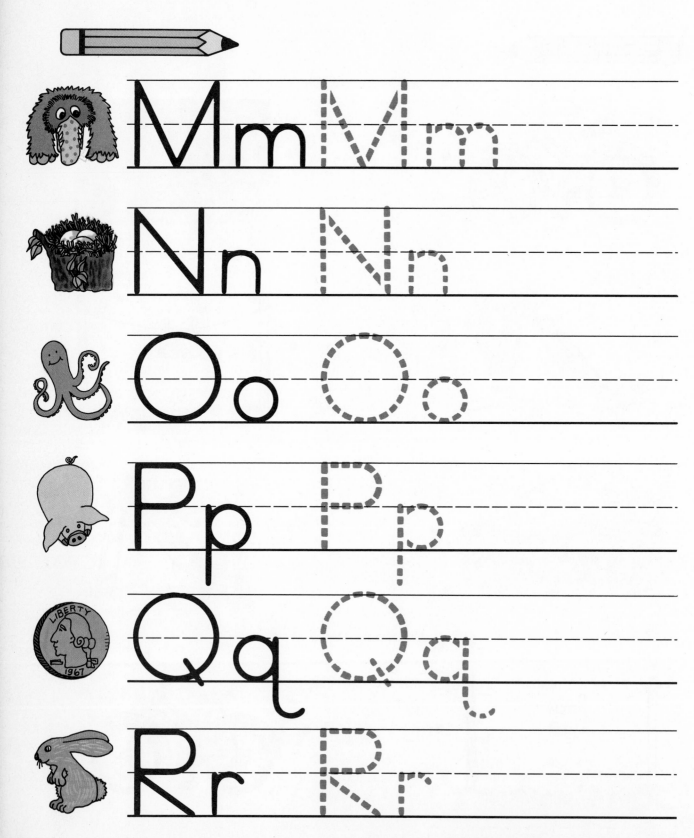

Unit 5
Study Skills

Children identify, trace, and copy upper- and lower-case letters.

10 STUDY SKILLS
The Seasons of the Year

Children learn the names of the seasons and mark the
illustrations according to teacher's instructions.

Real and Make-Believe

Mr. Benn-Red Knight

by David McKee

1 LITERATURE
Real and Make-Believe

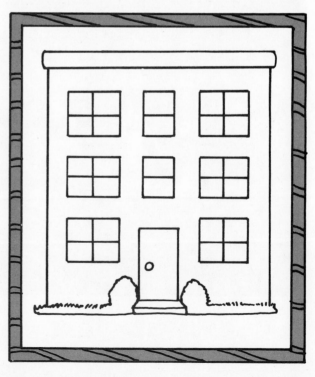

Children discuss illustrations and color those that picture things that are real.

Name

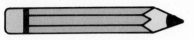

2 LISTENING
Drawing Conclusions

Children draw conclusions based on descriptions read
aloud and circle the correct pictures.

3 SPEAKING
Making and Using Puppets

Children create clothespin characters and use them in simple plays.

4 THINKING
Solving Problems

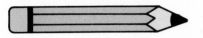

Children discuss problem situations and draw lines to illustrations of practical solutions.

5 WRITING PROCESS READINESS
Making a Book

Children follow steps of the Writing Process to draw parts of a story. They then dictate the story, or write it, using invented spelling.

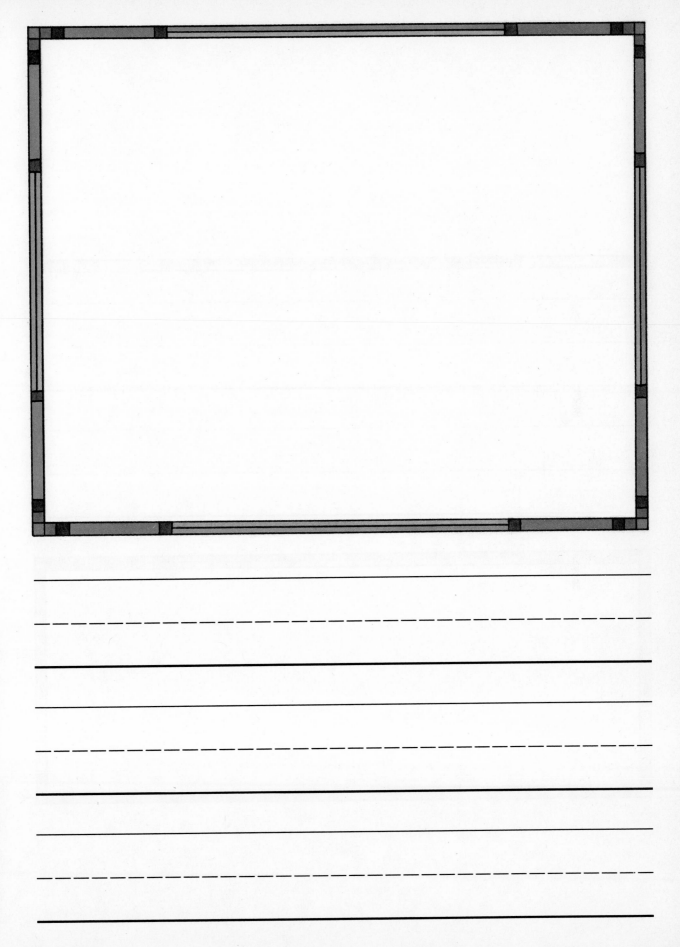

113

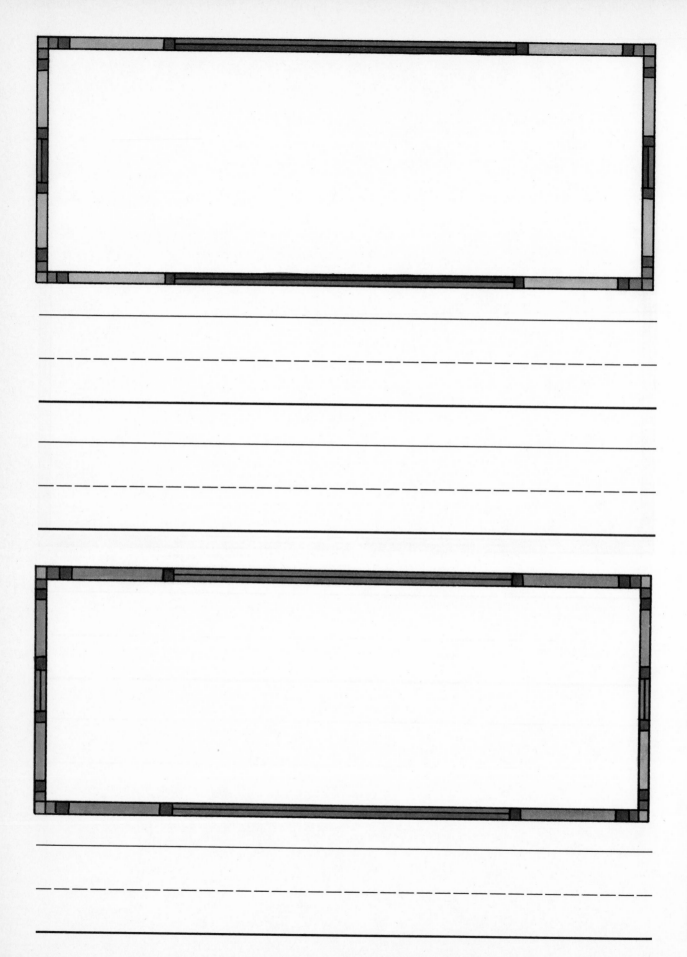

114

6 GRAMMAR
Describing Smells and Tastes

Children listen to words describing smell and taste. They
color pictures according to teacher's instructions.

7 GRAMMAR
Describing How Things Sound and Feel

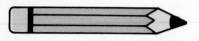

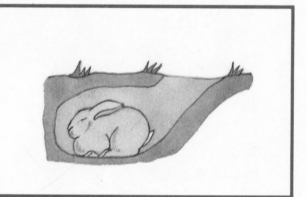

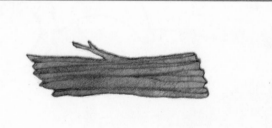

Children listen to describing words and mark the correct pictures according to teacher's instructions.

8 VOCABULARY
top, middle, bottom

Children color window curtains according to teacher's instructions.

Name

 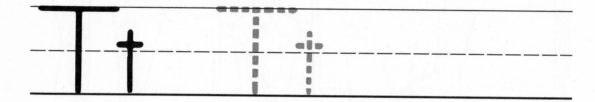
S s S s

 Tt Tt

 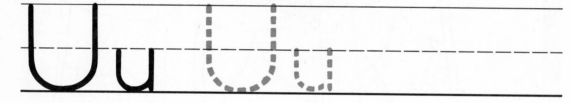
Uu Uu

 Vv Vv

 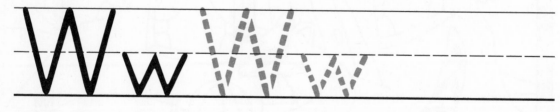
Ww Ww

Xx Xx

Children identify, trace, and copy upper- and lower-case letters.

Learning My Letters continued

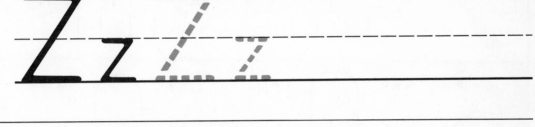

Children identify, trace, and copy upper- and lower-case letters.

10 STUDY SKILLS
ABC Order

Children connect the dots in alphabetical order to complete a picture.

Name

Picture Dictionary

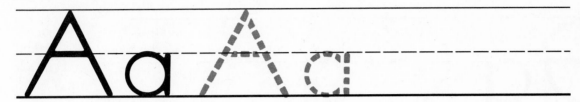
apple

Bb Bb Bb

boot

Cc Cc

cat

Dd Dd Dd

duck

Ee Ee

egg

Children identify, trace, and copy upper- and lower-case letters.

F f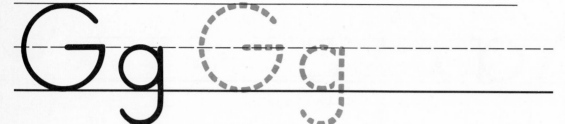

feather

G g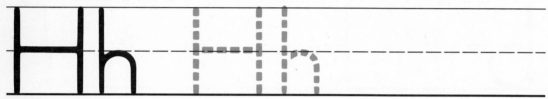

ghost

H h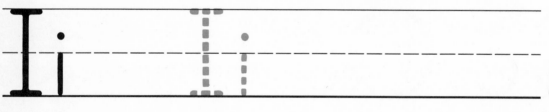

hat

I i

igloo

J j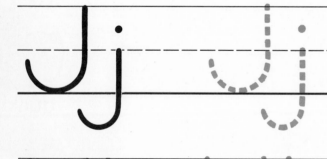

jack-in-the-box

K k

kite

Children identify, trace, and copy upper- and lower-case letters.

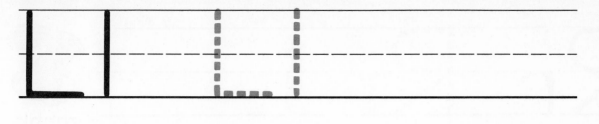

lamp

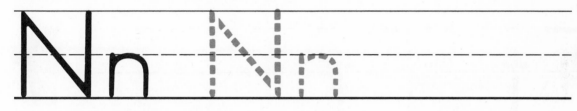

monster

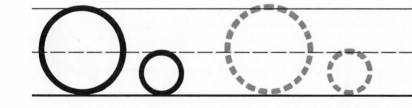

nest

octopus

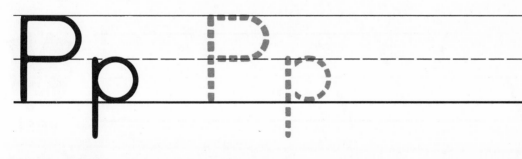

pig

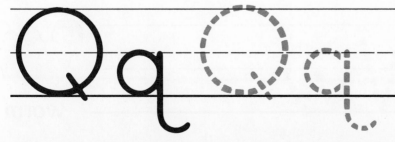

quarter

Children identify, trace, and copy upper- and lower-case letters.

R r   R r R r
rabbit

S s   S s S s
sock

T t   T t T t
tiger

U u   U u U u
umbrella

V v   V v V v
vest

W w   W w W w
worm

Student's Resource Book
Picture Dictionary

Children identify, trace, and copy upper- and lower-case letters.

Name _____

X x   X x   X x

Y y   Y y   Y y
yo-yo

Z z   Z z   Z z
zipper

Children identify, trace, and copy upper- and lower-case letters.

Name

Colors

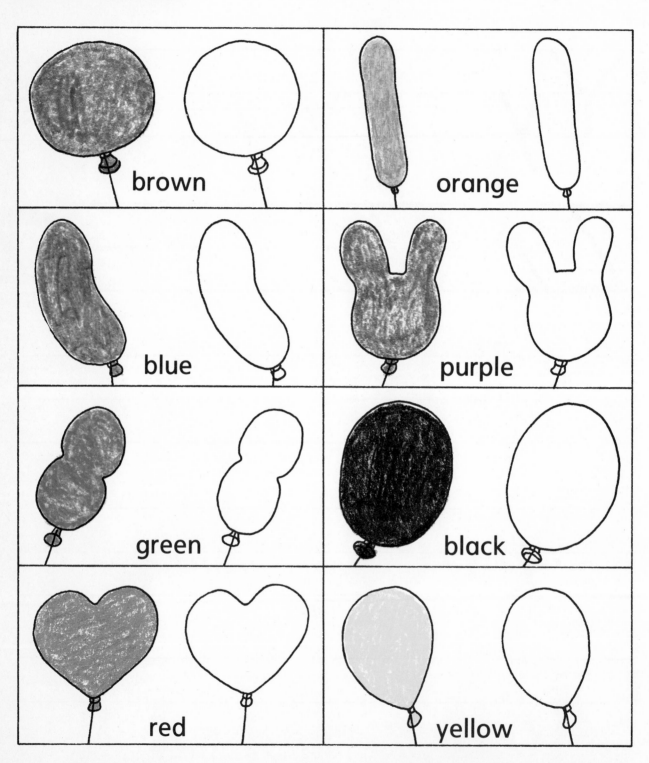

brown

orange

blue

purple

green

black

red

yellow

Children color the pictures according to teacher's directions.

Index

Numbers in **bold type** indicate pages where skills are taught. Names in italics refer to the punchouts at the back of the pupil book.

Adjectives
  comparing with, **102**
  that describe color, 29, **101**, 126
  that describe emotions, **64**
  that describe shape, **101**
  that describe size, **101**
  that describe smell, **115**
  that describe sounds, **116**
  that describe taste, **115**
  that describe texture, **116**
Agreement, subject-verb, 88
Alphabetical order, 120, 121–125
Antonyms, 103

Books, making, 9, 23, **98–100,** 112–114

Cause and effect, 97
Character, 42
Choral speaking, 96
Classifying
  by color, **60**
  by purpose, 27, 35, **83,** *Classifying Game*
  by shape, **60**
Color, 29, 60, 101, **126**
Comparing
  with adjectives, **102**
  recognizing likenesses and differences, **45–46,** *Same-Different Puzzles*
Conclusions, drawing, 109
Creative writing, 47, 61, 72, 84, 98–100, 112–114
Critical thinking
  classifying, 27, 35, **60, 83,** *Classifying Game*
  drawing conclusions, **109**
  recognizing causes and effects, **97**
  recognizing likenesses and differences, **45–46,** *Same-Different Puzzles*
  recognizing sequence, **71,** *First-Next-Last Game*
  solving problems, **111**

Describing
  color, **101,** 126
  a picture, **61**
  shape, **101**
  size, **101**
  smell, **115**
  sounds, **116**
  taste, **115**
  texture, **116**
Details
  adding to a picture, 47
  listening for specific, 95
Dictionary, picture, 121–125
Differences, distinguishing likenesses and, 45–46, *Same-Different Puzzles*
Directions
  following one-step, **43**
  following picture, 23, 77, 98, 110, 112
  following three-step, 9, 11, 13, 15, 17, 19, 21, 23, 27, 31, 33, 35, 37, 69
  following two-step, 7, 25, 29, 57
Discussions, 44, 49, 51, 70, 77, **82,** 89, 98, 102, 108, 110, 111, 112
Dramatic activities, 21, **96, 110**

Ending a story, 72

Information, listening for, 58

Left and right, 65, *Left-Right Game*
Letters, of the alphabet
  in a dictionary, **121–125**
  in order, **120,** 121–125
  tracing and writing
    A–F, **76,** 121–122
    G–L, **90,** 122–123
    M–R, **104,** 123–124
    S–Z, **118–119,** 124–125
Life skills
  solving problems, **111**
  using the telephone, **44**
Listening
  for context clues, 59
  critical
    to draw conclusions, **109**
    to predict outcome, **81**

  to follow directions
    one-step, **43**
    three-step, 9, 11, 13, 15, 17, 19, 21, 23, 27, 31, 33, 35, 37, **69**
    two-step, 7, 25, 29, 57
  for information, **58**
  to questions, 50
  for specific details, 95
  to telling sentences, 48
Literature
  skills
    distinguishing real from make-believe, **108**
    identifying characters, **42**
    listening for rhyme, **56**
    listening for sound words, **94**
    recalling story sequence, **68**
    recalling story setting, **80**
  types
    fiction
      "The Blanket That Had to Go" by Nancy Evans Cooney, 67
      "Jamaica's Find" by Juanita Havill, 41
      "Mr. Benn-Red Knight" by David McKee, 107
      "Tikki Tikki Tembo" retold by Arlene Mosel, 79
    poetry
      "A House Is a House for Me" by Mary Ann Hoberman, 93
      "Over in the Meadow," 55

Motor skills, fine, 7, 9, 11, 13, 15, 17, 19, 21, 23, 25, 27, 29, 31, 33, 35, 37

Nouns
  for animals, 21, 25, 27, **63**
  for people, 27, **62**
  for places, 27, **73**
  plural, **74**
  singular, **74**
  for things, 19, 27, 35, **73**
Numbers, 33

Onomatopoeia, 94

Order
alphabetical, **120,** 121–125
words, **71,** *First-Next-Last Game*
Outcome, predicting, 81

Pictures
adding details to, 47
using to follow directions, 23, 77, 98, 110, 112
Places, discussing, 27, 82
Plural nouns, 74
Poetry
"A House Is a House for Me," 93
"Over in the Meadow," 55
Positional Words
behind, 75
beside, 75
between, 75
bottom, 117
in, 52
in front of, 75
left, 65
middle, 117
on, 52
over, 52
right, 65
top, 117
under, 52
Predicting an outcome, 81
Problems, solving, 111
Puppets, 21, 110

Real and make-believe, 108
Rhyme, 56

Same and different, 45–46, *Same-Different Puzzles*
Seasons, 105
Sentences
completing, **59**
context clues in, 59
listening to
questions, 50
telling sentences, **49**
questions
listening to, 50
using, **51**
statements
listening to, **48**
using, **49**
Sequence
putting pictures in, 9, 23, **71,** *First-Next-Last Game*
recalling story, 68

Setting, 80
Shapes, 17
Signs, 11, 53
Singular nouns, 74
Speaking
choral, 96
creative dramatics, 21, **110**
discussions, 44, 49, 51, 70, 77, **82,** 89, 98, 102, 108, 110, 111, 112
non-verbal communication, 11, 53
story telling, 70
on the telephone, **44**
Story
characters, **42**
completing, **72**
drawing a, 61, 84, 98–100, 112–114
recalling sequence in, **68**
recalling setting of, **80**
telling, 70
Study skills
following picture directions, 23, 77, 98, 110, 112
identifying seasons, **105**
learning letters of the alphabet, 76, 90, **104,** 118–119, 121–125
left and right, **65,** *Left-Right Game*
practicing for a test, **91**
recognizing alphabetical order, **120**
recognizing signs, 11, **53**

Telephone, using, 44
Tests, practicing for, 91
Thinking skills
classifying, 27, 35, **60, 83,** *Classifying Game*
recognizing cause and effect, **97**
recognizing likenesses and differences, 45–46, *Same-Different Puzzles*
recognizing sequence, **71,** *First-Next-Last Game*
solving problems, **111**
Time words
first, next, last, **71,** *First-Next-Last Game*
yesterday, today, tomorrow, **89**

Usage
adjective, 29, **101, 102, 115, 116,** 126
agreement, subject-verb, **88**

Verbs
agreement with subject, **88**
identifying, 85, 86, **87**
matching, **87**
using in sentences, **88**
Visual discrimination, 25, 29, 45–46, *Same-Different Puzzles, Left-Right Game*
Visual memory, 13, *First-Next-Last Game*
Vocabulary
antonyms, **103**
that describes emotions, **64**
positional words, 52, 65, 75, **117**
time words, 71, **89**

Words
positional, 52, 65, 75, **117**
sound, **94**
time, **71, 89**
Writing Process Readiness
adding details, 47
completing a story, 72
drawing and describing, 61
drawing and dictating a personal story, 84, 98–100
drawing and dictating a make-believe story, 112–114
making a book, 9, 23, 98–100, 112–114